Science Vocabulary Readers

Incredible Owls

Justin McCory Martin

SCHOLASTIC INC.

NEW YORK • TORONTO • LONDON • AUCKLAND • SYDNEY
MEXICO CITY • NEW DELHI • HONG KONG • BUENOS AIRES

ISBN: 0-439-87637-0

Photo Credits

Cover: © Dwight Kuhn; title page: © Dwight Kuhn; contents page, top: © Millard Sharp/Photo Researchers; contents page, middle: © Martin Harvey/DRK Photo; contents page, bottom: © John Gerlach/DRK Photo; page 4: © Millard Sharp/Photo Researchers; page 5: © Michael Durham/DRK Photo; page 6: © Dwight Kuhn; page 7: © Arthur Morris/Visuals Unlimited; page 8: © Martin Harvey/DRK Photo; page 9: © Kim Taylor/Bruce Coleman; page 10: © Jack Michanowski/Visuals Unlimited; page 10, inset: © D. Cavagnaro/Visuals Unlimited; page 11: © Dwight Kuhn; page 11, inset: © Dwight Kuhn; page 12: © Art Wolfe/Photo Researchers; page 13: © Michael Giannechini/Photo Researchers; page 13, inset: © Edgar Jones/Bruce Coleman; page 14: © Michael Quinton/Visuals Unlimited; page 15: © John Gerlach/DRK Photo; back cover: © Dwight Kuhn.

Photo research by Amla Sanghvi
Design by Holly Grundon

15 14 13   12 13 14 15 16/0

Printed in the U.S.A.   40
First printing, September 2006

Contents

Chapter 1

What Is an Owl?

Owls are incredible! This book will tell you all about these very special birds.

The snowy owl lives in the chilly Arctic.

There are more than 200 kinds of owls. They live all over the world.

Fun Fact

Owls can turn their heads $3/4$ of the way around.

Owls have huge eyes. This helps them to see really well at night.

These look like ears, but they are just feathers.

An owl's ears are hidden on the sides of its head.

Owls have great hearing. They can even hear a mouse squeak half a mile away!

Chapter 2

Owl Life

Most owls rest during the day. Some sleep in old barns. Others snooze in the holes in trees or cactuses.

Owls are nocturnal (nok-**tur**-nuhl) **animals. That means they are active at night.**

Many owls wake up at night and call out to other owls. Some say, "Who, who!" Others **screech** or sing.

Up close an owl's feathers look like this.

Owls have very fluffy wings. This makes them silent fliers and helps them sneak up on **prey**.

Owls catch food with their sharp claws.

What do owls like to eat? Some eat bugs or lizards or frogs. Others munch snakes or rabbits or mice.

Chapter 3

Baby Owls

An owl's home is called a roost.

Most owls have babies in the spring. Many owls don't build their own nests. Instead, they move into nests left behind by other birds.

Most owl mothers lay one to twelve eggs. Owl eggs look like this.

Mother owls lay eggs. Then they sit on the eggs and wait and wait. It takes about a month for most owl babies to hatch.

Baby owls are called owlets.

Baby owls use their little beaks to break out of eggs. Peck, peck, peck! Here they come!

Fun Fact

Some owls can live to be 30 years old or more.

A mother owl takes good care of her owlets. She brings them food. She teaches them how to survive and communicate. "Who, who!"

Glossary

nocturnal (nok-**tur**-nuhl): to be active at night

owlet (**oul**-let): a baby owl

prey (**pray**): an animal that is hunted by another animal for food

roost (**roost**): the home of an owl

screech (**skreech**): a high, ugly sound

snowy owl (**snoh**-ee oul): a large, white owl that lives in the Arctic

Comprehension Questions

1. Can you name one thing that you learned about owl senses?

2. Can you name two things that you learned about owl homes?

3. Can you name three things that you learned about owl babies?